P9-EAJ-033

planting seeds

PAIRED:

Two idealists who would stop at nothing to help heal the world. Paul Farmer was struck by the poverty in Haiti and devoted his life to bringing health care to the poor. Wangari Maathai refused to accept limits set on women in her country and set out to transform Kenya's politics and environment.

"Anybody can learn to be interested in public service, or service to others. You could be 80 years old, you could be 20. You can still get engaged in service to other people."

Paul Farmer

"[Young people] have the energy and creativity to shape a sustainable future. To the young people I say, you are a gift to your communities and indeed the world. You are our hope and our future."

Wangari Maathai

Photographs © 2012: Alamy Images: 72 (Furlong Photography), 61 (David Keith Jones/Images of Africa Photobank), 70 (Marion Kaplan), 76 (Jake Lyell), 64 (Ariadne Van Zandbergen); AP Images: 49 (Ricardo Arduengo), 46 (Gregory Bull), 100 (Kike Calvo), 52 (Laurent Gillieron/Keystone); Corbis Images: 44, 96, 97 (William Campbell), 92 (Antony Njuguna/Reuters), 54 (Micheline Pelletier), 78 (Wendy Stone); Getty Images: 84 (William F. Campbell/Timepix/Time & Life Pictures), back cover right, 3 right (Gianluigi Guercia/AFP), 58 (Simon Maina/AFP), 67 (Priya Ramrakha/Time & Life Pictures); Magnum Photos/Peter van Agtmael: 40; NASA: 56 (Goddard Space Flight Center/NASA's Space Observatory), 14 (SRTM); NEWSCOM: back cover left, 3 left (Gary Coronado/Palm Beach Post/ZUMA Press), 26 (E.A. Ornelas/San Antonion Express/ ZUMA Press), 38 (p77/ZUMA Press), 10, 12, 18, 24 (s70/ZUMA Press), 32, 34 (Daniel Wallace/St. Petersburg Times/PSG); Reuters: 82 (Wairimu Gitahi), 98 (Yves Herman/Reuters); ShutterStock, Inc.: cover background (Richard Laschon), cover background (Kirsty Pargeter), cover (Smit), cover background (vectorgirl).

Illustrations by CCI: 56; Sophie Rasul: 14

Library of Congress Cataloging-in-Publication Data

Parks, Anna.
Planting seeds / Anna Parks & Ben Hewitt.
p. cm. -- (On the record)
Includes bibliographical references and index.
ISBN 13: 978-0-531-22559-2
ISBN 10: 0-531-22559-3
1. Maathai, Wangari--Juvenile literature. 2. Tree planters (Persons)--Kenya--Biography--Juvenile literature. 3. Women philanthropists--Kenya--Biography--Juvenile literature.
4. Environmentalists--Kenya--Biography--Juvenile literature. 5. Feminists--Kenya--Biography--Juvenile literature. 6. Farmer, Paul, 1959---Juvenile literature. 7. Philanthropists--United States-
-Biography--Juvenile literature. 8. Physicians--United States--Biography--Juvenile literature. 9. Poor--Medical care--Juvenile literature. 10. Partners in Health (Organization)--Juvenile literature.
I. Hewitt, Ben. II. Title.
SB63.M22P27 2012
333.72092'26762--dc22
2011009028

Tod Olson, Series Editor
Marie O'Neill, Creative Director
Curriculum Concepts International, Production
Thanks to Candy J. Cooper

Copyright © 2012 by Scholastic Inc.

planting seeds

Who says you can't change the world?

Anna Parks and Ben Hewitt

Contents

A HEALTHY OBSESSION: Paul Farmer

1 **A Stupid Death** 12

2 **The Blue Bird Inn** 18

3 **Healing Power** 26

4 **Beating Tuberculosis** 34

5 **Going Global** 40

6 **Scenes from Hell** 46

WOMAN WARRIOR: Wangari Maathai

7 **Tree of Life** 56

8 **Education of a Woman** 64

9 **A Green Belt** 72

10 **Behave, Women!** 78

11 **Democracy Now** 84

12 **A Prize for Peace** 92

Conversations with the Authors 102

What to Read Next 106

Glossary 108

Metric Conversions 109

Sources 110

Index 112

A HEALTHY OBSESSION

Paul Farmer fell in love with a country where people slept on dirt floors, drank unclean water, and lost their children to disease. Then he set out to make sure that no one else would ever die there just because they couldn't afford a cure.

Paul Farmer works on a letter at his home in Cange, Haiti. Farmer works 20-hour days in his quest to improve health care in Haiti and other poor nations. "I can't sleep," he says. "There's always somebody not getting treatment. I can't stand that."

1
A Stupid Death

Paul Farmer was desperate. He was 23, just out of college, and he had come to Haiti to help deliver medical care to the poor. Now the life of a pregnant mother of five was in his hands.

Farmer dashed through the halls of a run-down hospital in the town of Leogane, pleading with strangers for money. The woman waited in another room, feverish and shaking with chills. She had an advanced case of malaria and needed an emergency blood transfusion.

Haiti by Satellite

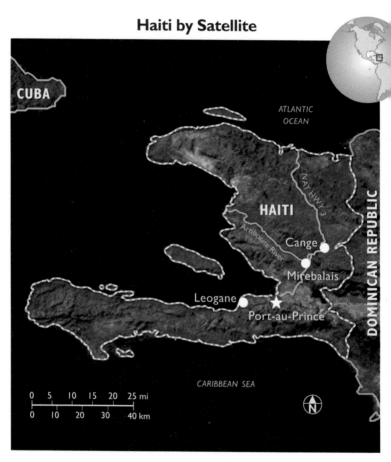

Haiti shares the island of Hispaniola with the Dominican Republic. Haiti is the poorest nation in the Western Hemisphere. More than 70 percent of Haitians live on two dollars a day or less.

In many countries, that would have been easy to provide. But this was Haiti, one of the poorest nations in the world. The hospital had no blood bank. And the dying woman had no health insurance. The woman's sister would have to travel 18 miles to Port-au-Prince to buy blood. But, like most people in Haiti, she was penniless.

Farmer was fresh from Duke University. He had majored in medical anthropology, studying the way a country's culture affects its health care system. In the process he had become fascinated by Haiti. Now he had moved there for a year to volunteer in hospitals and clinics while he figured out what to do with his life.

During his frantic race through the hospital, Farmer collected $15. The sister set out with the cash. But after paying for a round trip on a *tap tap*, one of Haiti's rickety public buses, she didn't have enough money left for blood. She returned with nothing.

"You can't even get a blood transfusion if you're poor," she sobbed.

Without the transfusion, the young mother lapsed into a coma. Within days she died, and her unborn child was lost. It was what Haitians called a "stupid death," the kind that happens too often when poor people don't have access to medical care.

In the weeks to come Farmer was haunted by a phrase that the dead woman's sister had repeated like a mantra: "We're all human beings," she had said. "We're all human beings."

The tragic deaths led Farmer to a decision. "I'm going to build my own hospital," he vowed. Doctors there would treat everyone. They would take in every beggar on the street, every lame, feverish person, no matter how poor or how sick. All of them were *human beings*, as deserving of a doctor's care as any billionaire.

In the young mother's death, Farmer began to see his future. Health care should not exist as a commodity to be bought and sold like a car. It should be an undeniable right, like freedom of speech or the right to vote. Farmer would devote his life to this principle. He would attempt to deliver the highest quality of health care to the poorest people in the world. And he would begin in Haiti.

When Paul Farmer was a teenager, he lived with his family on this boat, the *Lady Gin*. "Eight of us lived for over a decade in either a bus or a boat," Farmer recalls. "When you grow up in those conditions, surrounded by affection but not having a lot of things . . . then you get pretty resilient."

Paul Farmer Jr., or "P. J.," as his family called him, was born in North Adams, Massachusetts, in 1959. He was the second of six children. His father, Paul Sr., worked as a salesman. He was a gruff and restless man whose strict parenting earned him the nickname "The Warden." P. J.'s sweet-natured mother, Ginny, was a farmer's daughter who stayed home with her children when they were young.

P. J. had plenty of unusual obsessions as a kid, and his father encouraged them all. In the fourth grade P. J. tried to start a herpetology club to study amphibians. When none of his classmates showed up, his father insisted that the family stand in as club members. P. J. presided over meetings dressed in a robe. He displayed his charcoal drawings of frogs and lizards and lectured his brothers and sisters on amphibian diets and mating habits. He always introduced each species by its Latin name.

In 1966 Farmer's father moved the family to Alabama in search of a better-paying job. He bought a giant used bus made by the Blue Bird Company. When he found a teaching job in Florida, he loaded the family into the "Blue Bird Inn" and moved. He parked in a trailer park outside of Brooksville, Florida, and the bus became the Farmer home.

The Warden wired the bus for electricity, but there was no running water. He replaced the seats with bunk beds. P. J. had a top bunk, where he did all of his studying.

The Farmers lived in the Blue Bird Inn until, during one vacation, the bus flipped over and was totaled. The family moved into a tent until the Warden bought a 50-foot boat with a hole in it. The *Lady Gin* became the new Farmer home, moored in a creek where the family bathed and washed dishes. They lugged fresh water from town in jugs. At night P. J. fell asleep to the sound of alligators growling.

P. J. grew into a quirky and brilliant teenager. He made up a private language with his friends. He organized food fights and starred on the "High Q" television quiz show. In 1977 he was elected president of his senior class and won a full scholarship to Duke University.

At Duke, Farmer discovered medical anthropology. He also grew interested in a branch of Catholicism called liberation theology. According to liberation theology, a Christian's first duty is to help the poor and the powerless.

One of Farmer's research projects at Duke took him to migrant labor camps in rural North Carolina. He met Haitian immigrants who were barely surviving on their meager wages. He threw himself into the study of Haiti, writing a long article on the migrant workers. Another paper, on Haitian artists, won him a $1,000 prize.

When Farmer graduated from Duke, he applied to medical school. Then he took his prize money and flew to the poorest nation in the Western Hemisphere.

Farmer spent 1983 roaming throughout Haiti. He found volunteer work at an eye clinic in the town of Mirebalais, some 40 miles northeast of Port-au-Prince. Mirebalais lies in the middle of the Central Plateau, one of the poorest regions in Haiti. Only one road, National Highway 3, connected the town with the rest of the country. It was the main route through Haiti, and it looked like a badly rutted wagon trail.

Rattling across National Highway 3, Farmer was struck by the scenes of tremendous hardship. Nearly 80 percent of Haiti's people live below the poverty line.

Haiti was also one of the most "water poor" nations in the world. Sewage systems were either poorly built or nonexistent. Dirty water, often containing human waste, carried diseases like hepatitis and typhoid. Water-breeding insects spread

Farmer navigates through a crowded roadside market on his way to visit a hospital in Haiti in 2009.

malaria and dengue fever. Farmer knew he had his work cut out for him.

At the eye clinic, Farmer became friends with another volunteer, Ophelia Dahl, an 18-year-old from Great Britain. In just a week the two outsiders became friends. They strategized about health care in Haiti. And they found comic relief in mango-eating contests that turned into slimy food fights.

Farmer immersed himself in Haitian culture. He mastered Creole, one of the country's two official languages. He talked to patients about their lives and their living conditions. He attended local religious ceremonies. And he worked at the hospital in Leogane where he would later vow to make Haiti his life's work.

A boy stands next to a shack in Cange. Before Farmer visited Cange, he thought rusty tin roofs signified poverty. "But," he says, "the absence of tin in Cange screamed, 'Misery.'"

3
Healing Power

Farmer returned to the United States with a vision for his life. Knowing he could accomplish more in Haiti as a doctor, he entered Harvard Medical School. But he did it on his own terms. Every chance he got, he packed up his textbooks and flashcards and set off for Haiti. He'd return to complete lab sessions and take exams. Classmates began to call him "Paul Foreigner." Professors couldn't object since Farmer aced every exam he took.

Farmer had decided to focus his efforts on Cange, a desperately poor town in the Central Plateau. In Cange, people lived in makeshift shacks. They slept 12 to a room on dirt floors with roofs made of banana fronds over their heads. Dirty rags plugged the holes against the rain. Disease spread through the town like an uncontained fire. Infant and juvenile mortality rates ran sickeningly high. Mothers died in childbirth. Orphans grew hungry and sick, and daughters resorted to prostitution to feed their families.

There was no doctor or clinic in Cange, and Farmer dreamed of creating his own medical complex. He envisioned an entire community health system that might serve as a model for other communities around the world.

Ophelia Dahl joined Farmer in Cange. With the help of local Haitians, Dahl and Farmer walked hut-to-hut, interviewing residents about their suffering. They learned that a quarter of the children in Cange were dying of disease.

As in many poor areas, the misery stemmed from the water supply. Three decades earlier, Cange had been a village of farmers living along Haiti's largest river, the Artibonite. The river had irrigated their crops on the valley floor. But a hydroelectric dam built in the 1950s flooded the valley, destroying farmland and houses.

When the water came, the residents scrambled up the parched hills that surrounded the new reservoir, Lake Peligre. They tried to grow crops and raise farm animals on the dusty slopes. For water, they climbed down the 800-foot hills, dipped jugs into the reservoir, and carried them back up. The water sat for days, creating a breeding ground for disease. Each year people got sicker and inched closer to starvation.

Farmer's goals became clear: "Clean water and health care and school and food and tin roofs and cement floors," he said. These should be birthrights, he insisted, as automatic as breathing.

Working with a Haitian priest named Fritz Lafontant, Farmer laid out his priorities. He would give vaccinations to all residents and build a decent sewage system to protect drinking water. Then he planned to train a group of villagers to identify disease and administer medicines. After that, a new clinic would be built in Cange.

In 1985 a wealthy Boston philanthropist named Tom White flew to Haiti to meet Farmer and see his work. White was disturbed by the sight of a malnourished child in a dirt-floor hut. "Put a tin roof on and pour a concrete floor," ordered White, who owned a large Boston construction company. "I'll give you the money."

With White behind him, Farmer began to realize his vision. In 1987, White, Farmer, and Dahl founded Partners In Health, a charity based in Boston that would fund the project in Cange. A sister organization, Zanmi Lasante—which means Partners In Health in Creole—was established in Cange. White donated $1 million to get the project off the ground. In a place with nearly nothing, a health care oasis began to take shape.

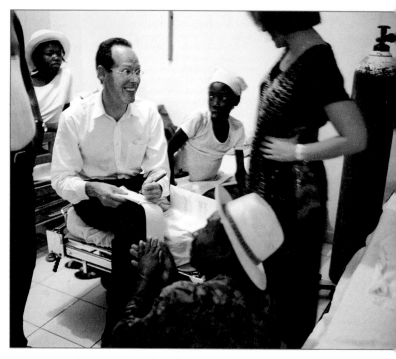

Farmer talks with patients and doctors at the clinic he started in Cange. Marta Cassmand (on the bed beside Farmer) has a rare but treatable form of cancer. She receives her treatment at no cost.

A few months later, a friend of Farmer's, Jim Yong Kim, joined PIH. Like Farmer, Kim was a medical student at Harvard. Farmer, Dahl, and Kim became a team, making plans late into the night.

And always, Farmer tended his patients in Cange. He had a way of folding his skinny frame around them like a grasshopper, one biographer said, of drawing them close. His manner alone—joking and reassuring, listening and touching—seemed to help people heal.

Farmer treated every patient like a family member. One man with AIDS had been shunned by people around him who were afraid of catching the virus. "When I was sick and no one would touch me," he told Farmer, "you used to sit on my bed with your hand on my head."

A crowd of patients wait to be seen by a doctor at Zanmi Lasante. People from all over Haiti travel by foot, donkey, or truck to receive care there. Zanmi Lasante currently employs more than 4,000 people, almost all of them Haitian.

4
Beating Tuberculosis

In 1988 Farmer was hit by a car in Boston and suffered a badly broken leg. While he was recovering, a woman at Zanmi Lasante died of tuberculosis, or TB. Farmer blamed himself for the loss. TB was entirely treatable, but he hadn't set the clinic up to succeed without him. The death pointed Farmer toward his next mission: devising a system that would bring effective care to poor people with TB.

Tuberculosis is a disease that feeds on poverty. It thrives where people live crowded together with poor ventilation—in slums, homeless shelters, prisons, and cramped rural huts. It spreads through saliva or mucus, when people cough or sneeze. An infected mother can wipe her nose on her sleeve and transmit the disease to her child. Weakened immune systems, caused by malnutrition or the AIDS virus, make people more vulnerable.

Many public health professionals claimed that TB was incurable among the poor and uneducated. Drugs were expensive, and patients often failed to take them regularly.

Farmer refused to give up on his patients. He designed a study that would give free drugs to two groups of people with TB. One group was given only the drugs. The other group received regular visits from health care workers to ensure that the patients took the drugs. This group also got about $5 a month to pay for food, child care, and transportation to Zanmi Lasante.

The results were powerful. Of those who received just the drugs, 48 percent were cured. In the extra services group, *everyone* was cured. Zanmi Lasante began offering the extra services to all TB patients. Over the next 12 years, not one patient would die of TB while receiving the treatment that Farmer designed.

Doktè Paul, as he was called, was helping to transform Cange. By 1989 he could walk to the top of a hill overlooking the village and see the progress. Water fountains gushed with clean water, ridding the village of malaria. New latrines had wiped out typhoid. The infant mortality rate was dropping. Many shacks now had tin roofs

Margarette Guerier Gracia (in straw hat), an employee of Zanmi Lasante, walks door-to-door in Cange. She distributes medication to people with HIV and teaches them about the proper use of the drugs and their side effects.

and concrete floors. Buildings that made up the new Zanmi Lasante health complex were appearing on the hillside, with more on their way.

This complex would grow into a hospital with a modern surgery wing, a blood bank, and laboratories. There would be a women's clinic, a school, a church, a kitchen to prepare meals for the hungry, and a center to treat TB.

But lasting improvements in Haiti were elusive. According to a Haitian proverb, *Beyond mountains there are mountains again*. The proverb inspired the title of a highly praised biography of Farmer, *Mountains Beyond Mountains*, by Tracy Kidder. For some, the proverb meant that conquering one obstacle merely allowed you to see the next one.

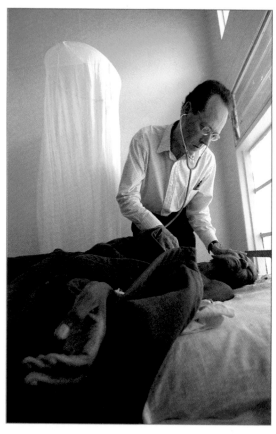

Farmer treats a patient at a Partners In Health clinic in a rural province of Rwanda, Africa. PIH opened this clinic in 2005, using the Zanmi Lasante complex as a model.

5
Going Global

Farmer's reputation grew as news of his success in Cange spread. He was known as a man who would do nearly anything to help his patients. When political turmoil made it dangerous to visit Haiti, Farmer simply ignored the danger and went anyway. And when medicines were hard to come by, he often smuggled them from the hospital where he worked in Boston.

"Better to ask forgiveness than permission," was Farmer's rule of thumb.

But despite Farmer's efforts, there were

always new obstacles—new mountains to climb. In the mid-1990s a man at Zanmi Lasante died of TB despite sticking closely to the treatment routine. Farmer identified the cause of death as multidrug-resistant TB, or MDR-TB. That's a form of TB that has developed a resistance to the usual TB drugs. The patient could only have been saved by a whole new set of medicines.

Farmer knew that this deadlier strain of TB couldn't be limited to a single case. Who knew how many other people in the Central Plateau had it?

Treating them wasn't going to be easy. Many people in the public health field argued against treating poor people who had MDR-TB. The medications were extremely expensive. And their results were mixed. There were only so many dollars to be spent on medical care for the poor, many argued. That money could be used more effectively in other ways.

Once again Farmer rejected the common wisdom. He and Kim persuaded the drug companies to lower prices. They gave the drugs to MDR-TB patients, along with the services they had provided for people with TB for years—food subsidies and visits from health care workers.

MDR-TB was eliminated in the Central Plateau, and Farmer had proven his point again: it was possible cure poor people if the other symptoms of their poverty were also addressed.

Partners In Health ballooned into a world-wide organization. Jim Yong Kim used the PIH strategy for treating people with MDR-TB in Peru. Farmer used it to help prisoners in the Siberian region of Russia.

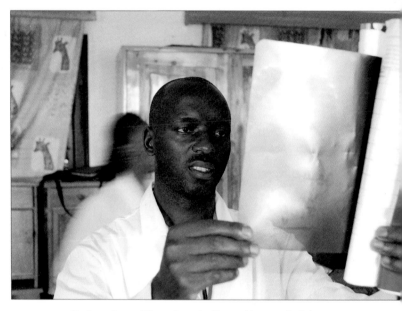

Dr. Jean Bosco Niyonzima studies an X-ray at Rwinkwavu Hospital in Rwanda, where he is chief of the medical staff. The hospital is co-run by PIH, which now works in 12 countries and employs about 13,000 people.

Later, the same methods were used to treat people with HIV and AIDS.

Farmer slowed down just long enough to start a family. He married Didi Bertrand, a medical anthropologist and the daughter of a Haitian schoolmaster in Cange. They moved to Rwanda, where Bertrand worked on a national health care program. Farmer spent time with his wife and three children between trips to PIH clinics around the world.

On January 12, 2010, Farmer had just left Haiti. He was in Miami, recovering from knee surgery. His phone rang, and a voice on the line said, "Thank God you're safe."

Safe from what? Farmer wondered.

A woman stands amid the destruction of her home in Port-au-Prince on January 13, 2010. Farmer says of the days following the earthquake: "From the beginning we knew there were no simple answers. We could tend to the injured, but what about the homeless? We could treat the sick, but what about burying the dead?"

6
Scenes from Hell

Just after Farmer left Haiti, a deadly earthquake had struck near downtown Port-au-Prince.

Farmer felt faint when he heard the news. Haiti was already so fragile. Poorly constructed buildings often collapsed on their own. Forests had been logged to near extinction. In 2008 four tropical storms had struck Haiti within four weeks, leaving it even more vulnerable to the earthquake.

On the third night after the quake, Farmer landed in a darkened Port-au-Prince.

Exiting the plane, he was overwhelmed by the stench of death. As he rode downtown, he saw collapsed buildings everywhere, no doubt with people still trapped inside. Bodies lined the roads, covered with white sheets.

It was a scene from hell. Farmer later wrote in a book, *Haiti After the Earthquake*: "It looked as if the heart of Port-au-Prince had been . . . bombed."

The enormous death toll could only be guessed at. "It's been a painful time for everybody who cares about Haiti," Farmer told a TV reporter, holding back tears.

Farmer did what he could to help the victims. Partners In Health staffed clinics in the tent camps that housed the homeless. By mid-February more than a million people were living in the camps.

Haitians work to free survivors from the remains of a collapsed building in Port-au-Prince the day after the earthquake. Two months later PIH announced a three-year, $125 million plan to rebuild hospitals and provide health care to more than 100,000 Haitians who had been displaced by the quake.

As the crisis dragged on, Farmer found hope in the success stories that came out of his clinics.

Carmene Geurrier was one of those stories. Geurrier had lost both legs in the quake. But with two prostheses supplied by doctors in Cange, she was soon walking, dancing, and playing soccer.

After Geurrier recovered, she became a paid community health worker. She hiked to visit patients with similar injuries, coaxing them toward recovery. "They ask me how I get to walk if my legs are hurting me, if I can do whatever I want with them," she explains in a Partners In Health video. "And I say, 'Yes.'"

Farmer and Dahl showed the video to a group in California. Then Dahl told the audience another success story—the kind that made all the travel, the late hours, and the heartbreak worthwhile. In the early days at Zanmi Lasante, a young woman in her ninth month of pregnancy collapsed at the clinic with an advanced case of malaria. Her condition was similar to that of the pregnant woman Farmer had watched die years before in Leogane.

But this time doctors treated the woman with anti-malarial drugs. She survived and gave birth to a boy who'd been "surely almost about to die," Dahl told the crowd.

The boy, Bobby, grew up. He went to medical school in the Dominican Republic. He will practice medicine in Haiti.

Paul Farmer, Ophelia Dahl, and Jim Yong Kim accept the Hilton Humanitarian Prize of $1.5 million in 2005. PIH was praised for providing "'first world' health care to the poorest societies, creating an innovative model that successfully has reversed the most devastating illnesses and returned people to productive lives."

Paul Farmer

Born:

October 26, 1959

Life's work:

Providing health care for the poor and fighting
infectious diseases

Day job:

Physician and anthropologist
Founding director of the organization Partners
In Health

Website:

www.pih.org

Awards include:

1993 MacArthur Fellowship
2003 Heinz Award in the Human Condition
2005 Hilton Humanitarian Prize
Countless honorary degrees and doctorates

Farmer's books include:

*AIDS and Accusation: Haiti and the Geography
of Blame*
Haiti After the Earthquake
Infections and Inequalities: The Modern Plagues
Partner to the Poor: A Paul Farmer Reader
*Pathologies of Power: Health, Human Rights, and
the New War on the Poor*

He writes:

"I have come to terms with the fact that [in
Haiti] I will never be asked to write, or even to
reflect overmuch on what is described in these
pages, because in Haiti I am asked to do only one
thing: to be a doctor, to serve the destitute sick."

WOMAN WARRIOR

She was beaten, jailed, and told to go home
and find a husband. But Wangari Maathai kept
fighting for her dream: a Kenya where women are
respected, forests are preserved, and no
one has to fear their own government.

Kenya by Satellite

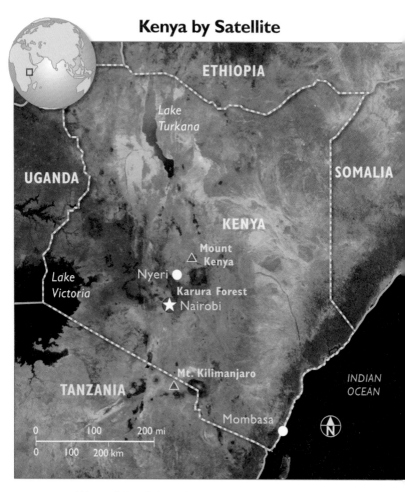

Wangari Maathai was born in a small village called Ihithe, part of the Nyeri district of Kenya. "At the time of my birth, the land around Ihithe was still lush, green, and fertile," she wrote.

7
Tree of Life

At the entrance to Kenya's Karura Forest, armed men surrounded Wangari Maathai* and her fellow protesters. As she told the story in her memoir, *Unbowed*, there were 200 or more thugs. They carried clubs, machetes, and swords.

"You can't get into the forest," the men told her.

"We're not trying to get into the forest,"

*She was born Wangari Muta. When she married, she changed her name to Wangari Mathai. Later, she changed her name to Wangari Maathai. Throughout this book, she is referred to as Wangari Maathai.

Security guards confront Wangari Maathai at the edge of Kenya's Karura Forest. Maathai was protesting a construction project that would have destroyed much of the forest.

Maathai said, forcing herself to stay calm. "We just want to plant a tree here."

"You can't do that," came the reply.

Maathai ignored them. She set the sharp point of her shovel against the ground and dug in. She would plant a tree.

The men closed in, shouting insults. "Who do you think you are, woman?"

It was a question that Wangari Maathai had been answering for years. In Kenya, Maathai's East African homeland, women were expected to stick to traditional roles. Girls rarely attended school. As adults, they had few career options. When they married, they were expected to do what their husbands instructed.

Maathai had chosen a different life. And

her choice had made her one of Kenya's most famous—and most effective—rebels.

On January 8, 1999, Maathai had gone to Karura Forest to do the work she had devoted her life to: defending Kenya's natural environment from human predators. The Kenyan government had just opened the public forest to private developers. The developers were preparing to clear-cut much of the forest and build expensive houses and fancy offices. The development would displace populations of monkeys, antelope, and birds. Deprived of their habitats, most of the animals would probably die.

Maathai and her small band of activists wanted to call attention to the threats facing the forest. They had invited news-

This forest in the Meru district of Kenya was slashed and burned to clear land for crops. Many forests in Meru have been illegally cut down by timber companies, tea planters, and potato farmers.

paper and TV reporters to accompany them. The event was organized around a single act: the planting of a tree.

It was a simple gesture. And yet, during the previous two decades, Maathai had used it as a powerful weapon against poverty and environmental destruction. She had mobilized thousands of women to plant millions of trees in Kenya.

As armed guards hired by the developers pressed in around her, Maathai pushed her shovel into the soil of Karura Forest.

Then the blows began to fall.

Maathai's group fled to a nearby police station, some of them limping on broken bones. Maathai was bleeding from a blow to the head.

At the police station, Maathai offered to take officers back to the forest to find the attackers. The officers refused. Instead they handed her a complaint form and told her to sign it.

Maathai put the tip of her finger to the wound on her head. She marked the form with a big red X, in her own blood.

A Kikuyu woman stands outside her home. Maathai was also a member of the Kikuyu, the largest of Kenya's 42 ethnic groups. "My parents were peasant farmers," Maathai wrote. "They lived from the soil and also kept cattle, goats, and sheep."

8
Education of a Woman

On April 1, 1940, Wangari Maathai was born on the floor of a small mud hut. The home had no running water or electricity. Like most rural Kenyans, Wangari's family was poor. They lived off the meager wages her father earned as a farm laborer. He worked on a large estate owned by one of the wealthy British settlers who occupied Kenya at the time.

Wangari and her family lived close to the land. They grew their own food in the fertile soil of the region. For fun, Wangari and her friends would go "mud skiing"—sliding down steep hills during Kenya's rainy season.

It was not a bad life, but Wangari's future was uncertain. Like most Kenyan girls, she was not expected to go to school. Instead, she would spend her days as most Kenyan women did: fetching water, cooking, and gathering firewood to prepare the family's meals.

But when she was seven, Wangari's older brother asked their mother a question: "Why doesn't she go to school too?" Her mother thought for a moment. She needed Wangari's help around the home, but she also believed in the value of a formal education. Her daughter, she decided, would go to school.

A Kikuyu woman teaches her class in a rural Kenyan school in 1966.

When school began that year, Wangari prepared for her future. Her parents had bought her a slate and a blank book for writing. She tucked them into a bag made from an animal skin. Then she set off barefoot down the dirt path to school.

Wangari excelled at her studies. She graduated from high school in 1959, one of the few Kenyan women to do so.

Most female high school graduates in Kenya took one of the two jobs generally reserved for educated women: teacher or nurse. But Maathai had her sights set elsewhere. In 1960 she won a scholarship to study in the United States. She went to college in Kansas and graduated with a degree in biology. Two years later she earned a master's degree from the University of Pittsburgh.

Now Maathai had to figure out what to do with her education.

Kenya had changed radically since she'd left home six years earlier. The country had declared its independence from Britain in 1963. A hero of the independence movement, Jomo Kenyatta, had been elected president. Under Kenyatta, the new government was looking for educated Kenyans to take over jobs that had been held by British colonists.

Maathai was offered a job at the University of Nairobi as research assistant to a professor of zoology. A letter of confirmation arrived in her mailbox in Pittsburgh. She was so excited that she skipped graduation ceremonies to return to Kenya.

That excitement stayed with her as she marched into the office of her new boss.

Jomo Kenyatta led Kenya to liberty in 1963 and became the first president of the independent nation.

But the professor hardly glanced at her confirmation letter. Instead he told Maathai that he'd offered the job to someone else.

"But you wrote me this letter," she protested. "I've come all the way from the United States of America." The professor just stared. The position was filled; there was no job for Wangari Maathai.

Maathai soon learned that the job had been given to someone who shared the professor's ethnic background. People from many different ethnic groups live in Kenya. Employers and politicians often favored people from their own ethnic group.

And, like the professor, the person who had been offered the job was a man. Maathai was learning a harsh lesson—even an education could not break down all barriers.

This photograph shows Nyeri, the district where Wangari Maathai grew up, in 1962. When Maathai returned to Nyeri in the 1970s, the forests in the district had been destroyed to make room for tea and coffee farms.

9
A Green Belt

Maathai was devastated by the loss of her university job. But she didn't stay discouraged for long. She got another position at the university and started working on a PhD in veterinary anatomy. In 1969 she married a businessman and politician named Mwangi Mathai. Two years later, she became the first woman in East or Central Africa to earn a PhD.

Then came a trip that would change the rest of Wangari Maathai's life. While doing research in the countryside, Maathai went to visit her family in Nyeri. She was shocked by how much the landscape had changed since she had left. Trees were disappearing everywhere she looked. Rivers were brown with soil from eroding fields and hills. The stream where she had collected tadpoles as a child had dried up. Even the people looked undernourished.

When she returned to Nairobi, she searched for an explanation. The government, it turned out, was encouraging villagers to plant crops that could be sold overseas. Many local farmers had stopped growing food to eat and started planting coffee and tea. Large plantation owners were clearing forests to plant cash crops. Timber companies had cut down native trees and planted exotic hardwoods to sell to builders.

Kenya was slowly being deforested—and people were suffering for it. Firewood for cooking was in short supply. Clear-cut hillsides no longer had tree roots to hold the soil together. The soil eroded into streams and lakes, polluting the drinking water. An entire way of life was dying in rural Kenya.

Maathai decided she had to do something, and she knew instinctively what it would be. She would plant trees.

The idea was simple, and yet there were so many ways it could help. Maathai would pay ordinary women a small fee to plant seedlings. The women would earn money and get involved in their communities. The trees they planted would provide wood and control erosion. New forests

Kenyan children carry firewood from the Kakamega Forest Reserve. Kakamega is the only remaining tropical rainforest in Kenya. It is home to more than 400 species of butterflies and many endangered animals.

would create habitats for birds and other wild animals. Fruit trees would increase the food supply.

Maathai called her plan the Green Belt Movement. "This land is naked, let's dress the land, make a belt," said Maathai. "A green belt!"

On Earth Day in 1977, Maathai and hundreds of her supporters gathered in Nairobi's Kamukunji Park. They carried shovels and young saplings. They sank the sharp edges of their shovels into the hard Kenyan soil. And there, in the middle of the country's largest city, they planted trees.

Most of the Green Belt Movement's leaders are women. They have planted more than 45 million trees in Kenya.

10
Behave, Women!

In the summer of 1977, things were going well for Wangari Maathai. She was a respected academic in Kenya. Her husband had been elected to the Kenyan parliament. She had just launched a movement that would provide work for rural women and protect the country's natural environment. Maathai was now a public figure and one of Kenya's most visible women.

Her public success, however, was destroying her private life.

Maathai came home one afternoon, just weeks after planting the first trees of the Green Belt Movement. She knew immediately that something was wrong. A pile of packing materials lay in the middle of the living room floor. All of her husband's belongings were missing. Mwangi Mathai had taken his things and left his wife.

To get a divorce, Mwangi Mathai went to court. At the time, divorce was not common in Kenya. He had to prove that his wife had been cruel to him or had committed adultery. He accused her of both.

Since Mwangi Mathai was a member of Kenya's parliament, the case attracted attention from the media. According to the Kenyan newspapers, he claimed that his wife was "too educated, too strong, too successful, too stubborn, and too hard to control."

The court ruled in Mwangi Mathai's favor, and the divorce was granted. Mathai also demanded that his ex-wife no longer use his last name, and she bristled at the insult. "I'm not an object the name of which can change with every new owner," she wrote. So she simply added an extra "a" to her last name.

Enraged by the ruling, Maathai told a reporter that the judge must have been either incompetent or corrupt. The judge demanded that she take back the comments. When she refused, she was charged with contempt of court and sentenced to six months in prison.

Maathai was loaded into a police van and hauled to jail. She was thrown into a maximum-security cell with four other women. A guard handed her a single prison blanket, which she folded into a square

A warden (center) watches two prisoners cook inside
Lang'ata, the largest women's prison in Kenya.
Maathai was jailed at Lang'ata for criticizing the
judge of her divorce trial.

to cushion herself against the cold concrete floor.

Three days later, Maathai's lawyer was able
to negotiate her release. But to Wangari
Maathai, the message was clear: "Every . . .
woman who contested her husband or the
male authorities was being told, 'if you try
to be anything but what you ought to be,
we will treat you exactly the way we have
treated her. So, behave, women!'"

But the experience did not make Maathai
more willing to "behave." In her memoir
she calls her time in jail a "turning point."
Up until then she had never violated the
law. Afterward, she says, she realized that
the justice system was not always fair.
She became determined to do what she
believed was right, no matter what the
personal cost.

President Daniel Arap Moi (in business suit) ruled Kenya for 24 years. He was a corrupt and violent leader.

11

Democracy Now

After her divorce, Maathai threw herself into her work with the Green Belt Movement. She often spent 18 hours a day in her office. The organization grew quickly. By the mid-1980s, nearly 2,000 women were planting trees and managing the nurseries that supplied the seedlings. Because of their efforts, millions of new trees were growing across Kenya.

But as the new seedlings grew, democracy in Kenya was dying. A new president,

Daniel Arap Moi, had taken over after Kenyatta's death in 1982. At first, Moi was popular with the Kenyan people. But just months after taking office, he banned all opposing political parties. After officers from the Kenyan air force tried to overthrow him, Moi cracked down even harder. He arrested hundreds of students who were accused of supporting the coup. He rounded up political opponents and put them in jail.

Like many people in Kenya, Maathai opposed Moi and his authoritarian leadership. She wanted a real democracy, with free elections and freedom of speech.

In 1988 Maathai took a stand against Moi. He was up for re-election, and she and other Green Belt workers started registering voters and demanding democratic reforms. On one level, their efforts came to nothing. Moi won the election easily, and most observers agreed that the vote had been rigged. The president announced that his party would rule Kenya for the next hundred years.

But Maathai was just getting started. "It would be only a matter of time," she later recalled, "before the government and I came into further conflict."

That next clash came in the fall of 1989. Maathai learned that the government was planning to build a skyscraper in the middle of Nairobi's Uhuru Park.

Uhuru Park was one of the few remaining pieces of nature in the city. Residents took walks in the park's forest. They picnicked on the grass and rode boats across a quiet pond.

The development threatened to devour much of the park. There were plans for a shopping mall and parking for 2,000 cars. The office building would be the tallest in Africa. The ruling party planned to move its headquarters there. And a giant statue of President Moi would stand guard over the entire complex.

Maathai immediately got to work trying to stop the development. She wrote letters, gave interviews, and talked to everyone she knew. Defenders of the project fought back. One member of parliament called her a "crazy woman." Others said the Green Belt Movement was a "bogus organization" run by a "bunch of divorcées." President Moi insisted that anyone who opposed the skyscraper had "insects in their heads."

But the movement continued to gather strength. As it did, many Kenyans gained confidence in their ability to challenge the government. Eventually the outcry was so strong that investors in the development began to pull out. Funding disappeared, and the project was canceled.

Maathai had won a major victory against the Moi regime. But the president made her pay. He ordered an investigation of the Green Belt Movement's finances. Then the group was kicked out of their government-owned offices. Maathai shifted the movement's 80 workers into her living room, two bedrooms, and garden.

The Uhuru Park fight had turned Maathai into a leader in the struggle for democracy in Kenya. And the movement was gaining strength. People across the country called for free and fair elections.

Moi's response was brutal. He vowed to hunt down democracy activists "like rats." At a protest in Nairobi in July 1990, his security forces fired into the crowd, killing dozens of people. Another demonstration in November 1991 was broken up when police attacked the protesters with rubber bullets and tear gas.

In 1992 Maathai and other political activists heard rumors that Moi was planning to put the army in charge of the country. According to their source, several of the pro-democracy leaders, including Maathai, had been targeted for assassination.

Maathai and her fellow activists went directly to the newspapers with the rumors.

The next day, ten police officers climbed Maathai's fence and surrounded her house. Maathai refused to come out. Instead she offered the officers tea.

The two sides settled in for a standoff. Maathai stayed barricaded inside her house. Journalists and friends gathered outside. Four police officers stood guard at the door. They bought milk for Maathai, and she passed tea out the window to them. Finally, on the third day, the officers broke in and arrested her.

For the second time in her life, Wangari Maathai was in jail. This time, she and several other pro-democracy leaders were charged with treason. If convicted, they could be sentenced to death.

Despite harassment from President Moi during the 1990s, Maathai continued her work with the Green Belt Movement. Maathai said her goal was "to persuade the leadership to be accountable, to distribute resources equitably, and to respect human rights and rule of law."

12
A Prize for Peace

Soon after her arrest, Maathai was released on bail. While she and the other pro-democracy leaders awaited trial, they received support from abroad. Several U.S. senators warned President Moi that relations with the U.S. would suffer if the prisoners were convicted. Not willing to risk his standing in the world, Moi gave in. In November 1992 all charges were dropped.

By that time, Maathai was already deeply involved in another protest. She had helped organize a group of women whose sons were in jail for opposing the government. The group camped out in Uhuru Park until the police chased them out with clubs and tear gas. Maathai was knocked unconscious during the struggle. The mothers took refuge in a cathedral. Out of respect for the church, the police refused to enter and arrest the women.

For an entire year, Maathai and the women slept in the church. Former political prisoners visited them and told of being tortured in the infamous Nyayo House, a government building in Nairobi. The stories leaked out to the newspapers, and Kenyans were shocked. The public revelations pushed Moi into a corner. Early in 1993 he released all but one of the 52 jailed sons.

During the mothers' campaign, friends warned Maathai to be careful. "I know that I am in danger," she told reporters during a trip to New York. "Because of the political turmoil in my country, one cannot rule out the possibility of the worst, so I do feel that I need to take care of myself. But that doesn't mean that I will not go back home. I will go home because that is where I am needed most."

When Maathai returned to Kenya, her fears seemed justified. She received death threats in the mail. Unmarked cars followed her through the streets. In 1993 she went into hiding for several months.

Gradually, however, Maathai began to feel safe in Kenya. She traveled around the world to speak at conferences and receive awards for her work with the Green Belt

Movement. She still had clashes with the government, including the beating she suffered at Karura Forest in 1999, when she signed the police form with her own blood. But Maathai had become too well known around the world for the government to get away with more serious attacks.

Besides, democratic reforms were transforming Kenya. In 2002 Maathai won a seat in the parliament. That same year,

In addition to protecting the environment, members of the Green Belt Movement fight for democracy and human rights.

President Moi stepped down peacefully. Mwai Kibaki was elected president in a free and fair election. He gave Maathai a job as an assistant minister, overseeing the natural resources of Kenya.

Two years later Maathai received the Nobel Peace Prize. This prestigious award honors one person every year for helping to create a more peaceful world. In her

Wangari Maathai received the Nobel Peace Prize in 2004.
Here she's in Oslo, Norway, celebrating with her son,
Muta Mathai, and her daughter, Wanjira Mathai.

acceptance speech, Maathai remembered playing with frog eggs in a stream near her home as a child. She thought they were beads until they hatched into thousands of wriggling tadpoles.

"Today, over 50 years later," she went on, "the stream has dried up, women walk long distances for water, which is not always clean, and children will never know what they have lost. The challenge is to restore the home of the tadpoles and give back to our children a world of beauty and wonder."

Maathai died of cancer in 2011. But in more than 30 years of work, she made great steps toward restoring the beautiful world of her childhood. She enlisted 30,000 women to plant 45 million trees. In the process, she helped bring jobs to the countryside and democracy to one corner of the Earth.

Wangari Maathai poses with her book *Unbowed:
A Memoir* at the United Nations' Climate Change
Conference. Maathai was the first African woman, and
the first environmentalist, to win the Nobel Peace Prize.

Wangari Maathai

Born:
April 1, 1940

Died:
September 25, 2011

Grew up:
Nyeri, Kenya

Life's work:
Empowering women and restoring natural environments in Kenya

Day job:
Adviser on democracy, human rights, and environmental conservation

Website:
www.greenbeltmovement.com

Awards include:
1983 Woman of the Year Award
1991 The United Nations' Africa Prize for Leadership
2003 WANGO Environment Award
2004 Nobel Peace Prize

Author of:
The Challenge for Africa
The Green Belt Movement: Sharing the Approach and the Experience
Unbowed: A Memoir

She says:
"[The] state of any country's environment is a reflection of the kind of governance in place, and without good governance there can be no peace."

A Conversation with Author
Anna Parks

Q *What do you think motivates Paul Farmer?*

A I think Farmer is motivated by a deep empathy for the poor, and by a missionary-like sense of duty to assist people who are suffering. The source of anyone's passion is always a bit of a mystery, but certainly Farmer grew up around poverty and with parents who felt a similar compassion for people who lived without. And there are religious roots to Farmer's convictions. I always think family dynamics play a part, but those are hard to discern; maybe he was driven by a need to please his demanding father. He was certainly born with a gift—a big brain—that his parents cultivated.

Q *What effect did his unconventional childhood have on the rest of his life?*

A It allowed him to take risks that he barely knew he was taking. He had always lived outside of the norm so it was perhaps comfortable for him to continue to live outside of the norm. If he'd bought a house in a nice suburb and mowed the lawn every week and commuted to an administrative desk job for 40 years, now that might've felt risky to Farmer.

Q *What impresses you most about Farmer?*

A It's inspiring to see someone live his passion on a large scale. He believed so faithfully in his mission that he was willing to flaunt the rules at Harvard, risk his life in Haiti, and challenge the medical status quo with his experimental outreach for people with TB. That requires an ironclad sense of self. I'm also drawn to the goofy side of Farmer, the made-up words and silliness. It's the combination of, "Yes I'm saving the world, but let me just take a moment to act like a five-year-old and mash this mango into your cheek." I like that.

Q *Do you think it's worth investing your life in a cause like Farmer's at the expense of time spent with family and on other pursuits?*

A It's an agonizing trade-off, one that I think women are especially sensitive to, this idea of having to decide between work and family. Farmer has a partner in the same field and a family, but he travels constantly. What is it like to live without the day-to-day closeness and intimacy of family? Do colleagues and patients offer the same joys? It is priestly, on the one hand, his life of sacrifice. And look what he's achieved. But he has also sacrificed the chance to see his wife and children frequently. That's got to be tough on everyone, including Farmer.

A Conversation with Author
Ben Hewitt

Q *How did you do your research for this book?*

A I was not able to get an interview with Wangari Maathai before she died, but I read numerous books, magazine stories, and newspaper articles about her. Fortunately she was written about widely.

Q *What motivated Wangari Maathai?*

A She was motivated by people and also by the natural world. She recognized the critical link between a healthy environment and healthy people. In Kenya, where her work started, people are so dependent on their local environment. If too many trees are cut down, they can't build fires to cook food. If the soil is eroded, they can't grow food, and they go hungry. Maathai saw that by helping to protect and rebuild the environment, she could also help the people living in Kenya and beyond.

Q *Was there anything you found particularly fascinating that you couldn't fit into this profile?*

A I was fascinated by Maathai's selflessness. She was willing to place herself in grave danger to stand up for her beliefs. That is a rare quality, and one I really admire.

Q *Is there a cause that might motivate you to take the kinds of risks that activists like Maathai have taken?*

A Although Kenya is very distant from America, I think we have some of the same issues here. They just aren't as obvious. The degradation of our environment is a big one. I'm not sure I'd be willing to go to jail, as Maathai did, but my family and I have made lifestyle choices to help reduce our impact. For instance, we built our home to be powered by solar panels and a windmill, and we live on only the amount of electricity we can produce.

Q *What do you like about being a freelance writer?*

A I think the best part is that my work is always changing. I get paid to learn about something new each week, month, or year. I also really appreciate the flexibility. Although I work a lot of hours, I mostly get to choose when and where I work.

What to Read Next

Fiction

Behind the Mountains, Edwidge Danticat. (166 pages)
Thirteen-year-old Celiane keeps a journal as she prepares to leave a turbulent Haiti behind to join her father in the U.S.

Countdown, Ben Mikaelsen. (256 pages) *A young Maasai herder in Kenya and a teenage American astronaut disagree about everything as they talk over ham radio—but then they finally meet each other.*

Forest of the Pygmies, Isabel Allende. (304 pages)
Alexander, his grandmother, and his friend Nadia go on safari in Kenya. They soon become involved in adventure after adventure.

Our Secret, Siri Aang, Christina Kessler. (224 pages)
Namelok, a 12-year-old Maasai girl living in Kenya, is not afraid to question the traditional ways of her people.

Taste of Salt: A Story of Modern Haiti, Frances Temple.
(192 pages) *This novel follows two young people as they come of age in the brutal political climate of Haiti.*

Nonfiction

Kenya (Destination Detectives), Rob Bowden. (48 pages) *This book presents an introduction to the resources, people, geography, and economy of Kenya.*

Mountains Beyond Mountains: The Quest of Dr. Paul Farmer, a Man Who Would Cure the World, Tracy Kidder. (352 pages) *Kidder takes the reader on a personal journey through Farmer's life and work.*

On That Day, Everybody Ate: One Woman's Story of Hope and Possibility in Haiti, Margaret Trost. (168 pages) *Trost helped start a program to bring meals to Haiti's hungry. She tells the story of her journey and the stories of those she met along the way.*

Books

The Next Eco-Warriors: 22 Young Women and Men Who Are Saving the Planet, Emily Hunter and Farley Mowat. (262 pages) *This book tells the stories of young activists who are fighting for the environment.*

Partner to the Poor: A Paul Farmer Reader, Paul Farmer, edited by Haun Saussy. (680 pages) *The book presents the collected writings of Paul Farmer from 1988 to 2009, which cover subjects such as health care, anthropology, and poverty.*

Films and Videos

Taking Root: The Vision of Wangari Maathai (2009) *This movie includes new material, TV footage, and first-person accounts of the confrontations between the Green Belt Movement and its opponents in Kenya.*

Websites

www.greenbeltmovement.org
This is the official site of Wangari Maathai's Green Belt Movement.

www.myhero.com/go/hero.asp?hero=Wangari_Maathai_MAG
This website is part of the My Hero Project and has information and videos about Maathai.

www.pih.org
This is the website for Partners In Health, the organization co-founded by Paul Farmer. It explains the goals and history of PIH and offers ways to get involved.

topics.nytimes.com/topics/reference/timestopics/people/f/paul_farmer/index.html
Read a short article about Paul Farmer and click on the links to a wide selection of articles about his life and work.

Glossary

AIDS (AYDZ) *noun* a disease that destroys the body's ability to protect itself against infectious disease

birthright (BURTH-rite) *noun* a right or a privilege that a person deserves just for being born

blood transfusion (BLUHD transs-FYOO-zhuhn) *noun* the injection of blood into the body of someone who is injured or ill

cash crops (KASH KROPZ) *noun* crops that are grown to be sold, rather than consumed by the people who grow them

clear-cut (KLIHR-kuht) *verb* to cut down all of the trees in an area of forest

coup (KOO) *noun* a sudden takeover of the government of a country illegally or by force

elusive (i-LOO-siv) *adjective* very hard to find or achieve

hydroelectric (hye-droh-i-LEK-trik) *adjective* having to do with using water to create electricity

infamous (IN-fuh-muhss) *adjective* well known because of a bad reputation

machete (muh-SHET-ee) *noun* a long, heavy knife with a broad blade, used as a tool and weapon

mortality (mor-TAL-i-tee) *noun* the number of deaths in a certain time or place

regime (ri-ZHEEM) *noun* a government that rules a people for a specific period of time

resistant (ri-ZISS-tuhnt) *adjective* in medicine, used to describe a virus or bacteria that's gained the ability to fight off drugs that would normally kill it

rigged (RIGD) *adjective* controlled dishonestly to achieve a selfish outcome

sapling (SAP-ling) *noun* a young tree

slate (SLAYT) *noun* a small hand-held writing surface made of a thin sheet of slate rock

strain (STRAYN) *noun* in biology, a group within a species that shares a common quality, such as the ability to fight off a drug

tear gas (TIHR GASS) *noun* a powder that severely irritates the eyes, nose, mouth, and lungs

transmit (transs-MIT) *verb* to pass something from one person to another, such as a disease

tuberculosis (tu-bur-kyuh-LOH-siss) *noun* a highly contagious bacterial disease that usually affects the lungs

vaccination (vak-suh-NAY-shun) *noun* the act of giving someone a medicine that teaches his or her body to fight off a disease. Most vaccines need to be given to a person before he or she comes down with the disease that the vaccine protects against.

vulnerable (VUHL-nur-uh-buhl) *adjective* in a weak position, likely to be hurt or damaged

Sources

A HEALTHY OBSESSION

Mountains Beyond Mountains: The Quest of Dr. Paul Farmer, A Man Who Would Cure the World, Tracy Kidder. New York: Random House, 2004. (including quotes on pages 12, 16, 26, 30, 31, 41)

"Anderson Cooper: 'There's Just Stupid Death Happening Here Now,'" Lindsay Robertson. *New York*, January 16, 2010.

"Bedside Manner," Tracy Kidder. *Harvard Magazine*, November–December 2003.

"Dr. Farmer's Remedy," Byron Pitts. *60 Minutes*, May 4, 2008. (including quotes on pages 18, 40)

"The Good Doctor," Tracy Kidder. *New Yorker*, July 10, 2000. (including quote on page 33)

Haiti After the Earthquake, Paul Farmer. New York: Perseus Books, 2011. (including quotes on pages 45, 46, 48)

LinkedIn Speaker Series: Paul Farmer. YouTube.com, April 13, 2001. (including quotes on pages 50, 51)

"The Man Who Would Cure the World," Academy of Achievement interview with Paul Farmer. July 3, 2009. (including quote on page 4)

"Paul Farmer, MD, PhD," Harvard University Department of Global Health and Social Medicine website.

"Partners In Health Receives Humanitarian Prize." *Philanthropy News Digest*, September 28, 2005. (including quote on page 52)

Pathologies of Power: Health, Human Rights, and the New War on the Poor, Paul Farmer. Los Angeles: University of California Press, 2003. (including quote on page 53)

PIH.org Official website of Partners In Health.

WOMAN WARRIOR

Unbowed, Wangari Muta Maathai. New York: Random House, 2006. (including quotes on pages 56, 57, 59, 64, 71, 80, 81, 83, 87)

"Common Heritage, Diverse Interests: Deforestation and Conservation Alternatives for Mount Kenya," Joseph Kariuki. *Cahiers d'Outre-Mer,* July–September 2006.

"From the Ground Up: Wangari Maathai's Plan for Cultivating Peace Is Taking Root in Africa," Lynne Duke. *Washington Post,* December 26, 2004. (including quote on page 66)

"I Am Woman," Tami Hultman. *Africa News,* June 8, 1992. (including quote on page 95)

"Kakamega Forest National Reserve." Kenya Wildlife Service, 1996 and 2011.

"Kenya: Human Rights Developments." Human Rights Watch, 1990. (including quote on page 90)

"She Planted Trees—and Hope—in Kenya," Annette John-Hall. *Philadelphia Inquirer,* October 19, 2006. (including quote on page 77)

"That Mad Woman." *Noseweek,* December 2009. (including quote on page 92)

"Wangari Maathai: Nobel Lecture." Nobel Foundation, December 10, 2004. (including quotes on pages 5, 99, 101)

Index

AIDS, 33, 36, 45

Artibonite River, **14,** 29

Bertrand, Didi, 45

Cange, **14, 26,** 28–31, **32,** 33, 37, **38,** 41

clear-cutting, 60, **61,** 74–75

Creole, 25, 31

Dahl, Ophelia, 25, 29, 31, 33, 50–51, **52**

Duke University, 15, 22

Farmer, Ginny, 19, 21

Farmer, Paul, **12, 24, 32, 40, 52**

Farmer Sr., Paul, 19

Geurrier, Carmene, 50

Gracia, Margarette Guerier, **38**

Green Belt Movement, 77, **78,** 80, 85–86, **92, 96,** 96–97

Haiti, 12, 13, **14,** 15–17, 22–23, **24,** 25, 27, 29, 31, 39, 41
  earthquake, **46,** 47–48, **49,** 51

Harvard Medical School, 27, 33

HIV, 38, 45

hepatitis, 23

Jim Yong Kim, 33, 43, **52**

Kakamega Forest, Kenya, **76**

Karura Forest, Kenya, 57, **58,** 60, 63, 97

Kenya, **56,** 59, 75

Kenyatta, Jomo, 69, **70**

Kidder, Tracy, 39

Kikuyu, **64, 67**

Lady Gin, **18,** 21

Lafontant, Fritz, 30

Lake Peligre, 29

Lang'ata prison, **82**

Leogane, 13, **14,** 25, 51

liberation theology, 22

Maathai, Wangari, **54, 58, 92**
  as activist, 57, 59–60, 62–63, 86–91, 93–94
  childhood, 65–66
  education, 68, 73
  divorce, 80–81
  imprisoned, 81, 83, 91
  elected to parliament, 98
  Nobel Peace Prize, 98, **100**

malaria, 13, 25, 37, 51

Mirebalais, **14,** 23

Moi, Daniel Arap, **84,** 86–90, 93–94, 98

Nairobi, Kenya, 74, 77, 87, 90

National Highway 3, **14,** 23

Nyeri, **72,** 74

Partners In Health, 31, 33, 40, 43, 44, 45, 48, 49, 50, 52

Port-au-Prince, **14,** 15, 23, **46,** 47, 48, **49**

Rwanda, Africa, **40, 44,** 45

tuberculosis, 35–37, 39, 42–43

typhoid, 23, 37

Uhuru Park, Nairobi, 87–89

Unbowed, 57

University of Nairobi, 69

White, Tom, 31

Zanmi Lasante, 31, **34,** 35, 37, 38, 39, 40, 42, 51